Monetising Life Experience

Jack's Curated Business Idea

Jack Lookman

Monetising Life Experience

Jack's Curated Business Idea

Copyright © 2023 Jack Lookman Limited

A. ACKNOWLEDGEMENT

I continue to be grateful to my Creator and Sustainer, for known and unknown favours, protection and blessings.

I appreciate my parents, for being the vehicle of success.

I was fortified with spiritual and academic knowledge and practices; as well as great life skills.

Contributions of John Tosin Adekunle are much appreciated.

My beautiful Tolu Mayowa Tobi you are very much appreciated.

I appreciate all my Teachers, both formal and informal - Thank you very much.

To all those who've added value to me, I say, thank you.

To my Creator and Sustainer: Alhamdu lillahi rabbi alAAalameena.

jacksempowerment.com. jacklookman.co.uk. jaaloo.com

B. DEDICATION

This piece of work is dedicated to all my family members.

My Late Dad

My Mum

My Siblings

My Children

Ire awawa ri o. (May you find the blessings that you desire)

Ire aje'n jetan (May our Creator and Sustainer grant us everlasting blessings)

jacksempowerment.com. jacklookman.co.uk. jaaloo.com

Hello! Welcome to our series on Jack's Curated Business Ideas. My name is Olayinka Carew aka Jack Lookman. Today's topic is *Monetising Life Experience.*

1. Preamble

Are you someone with few skills? Are you an older citizen? Do you require additional income? Do you wish to reduce the burden on your children? Could you be a Content Creator? Do you require a side hustle? Do you wish to add value to society? Do you wish to explore latent skills? Could you be sitting on a pot of gold?

Could you leverage Social media? Will you love to think outside the box? Could you become impactful? Could you make a difference? Is that degree of life accumulating dust? Could you monetize life experiences? Could you monetize your life experience? Is your life experience a waste? Is your life experience accumulating dust?

Are you sleeping on gold? Is that far away dream right there by your side? Is it awaiting execution? Could you collaborate? Could you make it happen? Could you make hay while the sun shines? Or will you wait until after then, when the opportunity leaves? Could there be learnings for others?

Could you share your story? Could your story be anonymous? Do you need to be learned? Do you need to be successful? Have you made any little life wins? Have you succeeded where others failed?

Could pitfalls be avoided? Successes, failures, pitfalls? Good, bad and ugly? Is it original? Is it valuable? Is it interesting? Has it got great potential? Do you wish to monetize?

If yes, this project may be of interest.

Will you love to find how?

If you've answered yes to any or more of these questions, please continue consuming this content.

. jacksempowerment.com. jacklookman.co.uk. jaaloo.com

2. Youtube viewers

If watching this video on Youtube, it has timestamps. You could zoom into the sub-topics of interest.

https://youtu.be/wGoHxlLfrkQ

3. Introduction

I see different every day people; some with inspirational stories, stories which could inspire children and positively impact their lives. Stories which could impact their mindsets as well as expectations. Stories which could mould them into greater and better adults, but some of these stories are not told in the media or papers. They are not in text books and not taught in university. They are buried in sands of time, because the authors are not visible. Could this present an entrepreneurial opportunity? For the benefit of both parties? Could the story originator benefit as well as the content creator? Could society benefit as well as the world at large? Let's explore possibilities with the hope of answering.

4. Will the narration be anonymous?

Some of the content may be sensitive; there's however a need to share experiences to enable learning. Anonymity may be the way forward. Legalities shall be put in place to protect the identity of the narrator. That way, great content may be shared and the process may be richer.

5. Possible learnings from failure?

As negative as failure may seem, there are benefits, which may come forth; pitfalls to avoid, lessons from failure, and how the failure was overcome.

jacksempowerment.com. jacklookman.co.uk. jaaloo.com

6. Benefits of the Project

Some potential benefits from this project, include:

- Financial benefits
- Impact
- Empowerment
- Inspiration
- Fame

- Wealth

- Opportunity

- Jobs

- Skill enhancement

- Etc

7. Could this project become a cash cow?

If the content is well curated; if due diligence is applied; if the content is relevant and if well accepted. If the content is well marketed and if the project is blessed; you could make a lifetime of passive income. You could even monetize in your grave.

jacksempowerment.com. jacklookman.co.uk. jaaloo.com

8. Is there a need for collaboration?

To execute this project, you could do a solo effort or you could collaborate. Research and consider the pro's and cons and decide on the path that best suits you. There's the option of collaborating with narrators or collaborating with suitable others. You could profit share or you could pay them off. It's your judgement call to protect and manage your best interest.

9. Collaboration opportunities with Jack Lookman

Have you come across our products and services? Do they resonate with you? Will you like to have a chat? Could you add value to our doings? Could you benefit therefrom? Will you love to collaborate with Jack Lookman? If yes, please send an email to jacklookman@yahoo.co.uk

Use an appropriate subject heading and a brief narrative. We'll give your request due consideration by God's grace.

10. Collection of Experiences?

The content shall be:

- Concise

- Anonymous

- Easy to digest

- Of great value

- Be interesting

- And relevant

jacksempowerment.com. jacklookman.co.uk. jaaloo.com

11. Could you collaborate?

Yes, you could. You may be academic. You may be literate. You may be illiterate or semi illiterate; it doesn't really matter. What's important is to communicate the valuable life experience/s. The Content Creator and suitable others will do the rest

12. Could content be created on 1 or more platforms?

Yes, it could. On platforms such as:

- Ebooks
- Paperbacks
- Social media
- Blogs
- Vlogs
- Podcasts
- Etc.

jacksempowerment.com. jacklookman.co.uk. jaaloo.com

13. Could there be a template for the content?

This might be beneficial. It could make the process more structured. Give some thought to this, create your template and modify it as necessary.

14. Could the content be evergreen?

As long as the content is rich, as well as relevant and valuable, it could become an evergreen product. Yourself and generations could benefit financially and morally.

15. Expectation management / disclaimer

For this project, there is a possibility of success or failure. Nothing is guaranteed. Effort and time is required. Skills are required. Commitment is required. Acceptability by content consumers is required. Grace and blessings are required; etc

jacksempowerment.com. jacklookman.co.uk. jaaloo.com

16. What format will it take?

The content could be in one or more of these formats:

• Text

• Audio

• Video

• Animation

• Narrative

• Interview

• Etc

17. How could the project be funded?

It could be funded:

- Individually
- Via Family and friends
- Via Crowdfunding
- Via Bank loan
- Via Investors
- Etc

jacksempowerment.com. jacklookman.co.uk. jaaloo.com

18. How could life experience be monetized?

For the purpose of this presentation, you could monetize life experience by creating content. This could be on various platforms in different formats in different languages and for different audiences. You could monetize via:

- Product sales
- Adverts
- Marketing
- Sponsors
- Etc

19. Who shall own the intellectual rights?

This could be negotiated with concerned parties. Agreements shall be articulated. It could be jointly or singularly owned. Legalities shall be put in place to avoid conflict. The process needs to be fair. The aim is for a win-win by all concerned parties

20. Is life experience taught in the classroom?

The simple answer is no. Or may be, little. Different life and other experiences are captured on different media, textbooks, films, videos, Social media, verbal letters, novels, comedies, documentaries, etc. But these may only be a drop in the ocean.

21. Is there really a degree on life experience?

To get a degree, you may need to go to university; but life experience is much beyond university. There's no major script for it. May be more of guidance. For example, academics and professionals could fail at marriage. They could also fail at bringing up desirable children. Some academics may be bad cooks. Some may be unable to effectively manage money. Some may have poor domestic skills; relying on cleaners and cooks to keep the house. Some may only be academically inclined, but may not be street smart. Some crumble in the face of adversity and some are only good in their specialities. You therefore don't get all life learning in university.

On the other hand, life teaches lots of lessons, which could be informal.

If these are found to be worthy, we could hypothetically give a degree of life learning.

This could however be difficult to quantify; or couldn't it?

22. In what language should the content, be?

Consider: a single language; multiple languages; translations.

Though it's your judgement call, it's suggested to be in multiple languages.

This may however impact your finances and resources.

If the return on investment becomes much higher then it may prove a wise decision.

jacksempowerment.com. jacklookman.co.uk. jaaloo.com

23. Some legal considerations to ponder:

- Agreements

- Contracts
- Profit Sharing Formula
- Intellectual rights
- Ethics
- General data protection regulation
- Indemnification
- Anonymity - as necessary
- Etc

jacksempowerment.com. jacklookman.co.uk. jaaloo.com

24. Could there be any leveraging options?

Yes, there could. You could leverage your:

- Network
- Your skills
- Your wider network
- Freelancers
- The internet
- Social media
- Interpersonal skills
- Your experience

- Your exposure
- Your strengths
- Etc

25. Some marketing plan considerations:

- Budget
- Digital marketing
- Affiliate Marketing
- Social Media Marketing
- Influencer marketing
- Traditional marketing
- Advertising
- Referrals
- Outsourcing the marketing
- Managing the marketing process
- Etc

jacksempowerment.com.   jacklookman.co.uk.   jaaloo.com

26. Mentoring with Jack Lookman

Are you enjoying the content? Have you consumed other content by Jack Lookman? Do you resonate with content by Jack Lookman? Will you love to be mentored by Jack Lookman? Your age is unimportant, as learning is lifelong.

We could learn from each other.

Consider visiting jacksempowerment.com

Search for Jack's Mentoring 101

Or use this link:

https://www.jacksempowerment.com/products/courses/view/1152633

We have free and paid content if interested, please send a brief email to jacklookman@yahoo.co.uk

Use an adequate subject heading and a short narrative.

jacksempowerment.com. jacklookman.co.uk. jaaloo.com

27. Some thoughts on the methodology and process

- Interviewing the narrator
- Scouting for possible narrators
- Content creation
- Content editing
- Publishing on multiple platforms

- Quality control
- Marketing
- Profit sharing
- Monetisation
- Data capture
- Social media leverage
- Advertising
- Legalities
- Accountability
- Transparency
- Payment of 'royalties'
- Etc

28. Monetisation plan

- Product sales
- Platform monetisation; e.g Social media, etc
- Royalties
- Conversion to films
- Interviews
- Public speaking

- Platform adverts
- Private label rights
- Etc?

29. Some suggested niches

- Males
- Females
- Youths
- Students
- Undergraduates
- Graduates
- Widows
- University experiences
- Widowers
- Artisans
- Professionals?
- Villagers
- Under-privileged
- Elderly
- Retirees

- Journeys through adversity
- Survivors
- Orphans
- Illiterates
- Semi-literates
- Diasporas
- Etc

jacksempowerment.com. jacklookman.co.uk. jaaloo.com

30. Potential opportunities from the project

- Monetisation
- Wealth creation
- Job creation
- Impact
- Value sharing
- Societal enrichment
- Lingual enrichment
- Education
- Mailing list
- Marketing
- Re-marketing

- Enlightenment
- Skill enhancement
- Literacy enhancement
- Empowerment
- Inspiration
- Etc

31. At Jack Lookman Limited

Our mission is to Empower and Inspire Generations by leveraging the Internet.

Yes, it's about Empowerment and Inspiration.

jacksempowerment.com. jacklookman.co.uk. jaaloo.com

32. Who owns the intellectual rights?

- Narrator?
- Content Creator?
- Entrepreneur?
- Publisher?
- Social media platforms?
- Other publishing platforms?
- A combination of the above?

This shall be negotiated and articulated.

33. Some thoughts to consider are:

- Negotiations
- Legalities
- Fairness
- Profit Sharing Formula
- Royalty
- Compromise
- Joint ownership
- Etc

34. Could passive income be earned?

The content has potential of yielding passive income. You put in the initial effort and then carry out maintenance as necessary and of course marketing. Once the content is of great value, the business could become a cash cow.

jacksempowerment.com.   jacklookman.co.uk.   jaaloo.com

35. On which platforms could content be published?

Some considerations are:

- Social media
- Paperbacks
- Blogs
- Podcasts
- Ebook
- Television
- Radio
- Etc

36. Some Profit Sharing Formula considerations:

- Negotiation
- Fairness
- Legalities
- Royalty
- Payment dates
- Trust
- Accountability
- Transparency
- Payment methods

- Empathy

37. What resources are required?

- Human resources
- Equipment
- Narrator
- Platforms
- Positive mindset
- Relevant skills
- Empathy
- Transportation
- Etc

jacksempowerment.com. jacklookman.co.uk. jaaloo.com

38. Some scope considerations:

- Interesting content
- Great value
- Impactful content
- Original content
- Profitable content

39. Some suggested skills

- Storytelling
- Content creation skills
- Language skills
- Basic legal skills
- Communication skills
- Interpersonal skills
- Fundraising skills
- Budgeting skills
- Numeracy skills
- Basic information technology skills
- Social media skills
- Marketing skills
- Entrepreneurial skills
- Marketing skills
- Profit Sharing Formula skills
- Etc

jacksempowerment.com.   jacklookman.co.uk.   jaaloo.com

40. Could a team be of benefit?

An ideal team could include the undermentioned; however some individuals could carry out multiple activities.

Below are suggested team members:

- Content Creator
- Linguist
- Translator
- Legal personnel
- Social media personnel
- Marketer
- Entrepreneur
- Publisher
- Scout
- Driver
- Etc

jacksempowerment.com. jacklookman.co.uk. jaaloo.com

41. What exactly is the idea?

It's about curating beneficial content from interesting life experiences; especially from untapped sources, such as:

- The elderly
- The disadvantaged
- The deprived
- Professionals
- Common people
- Etc

It's about curating content, commercializing it, and profit sharing.

Internet, technology and Social media shall be extensively leveraged.

jacksempowerment.com. jacklookman.co.uk. jaaloo.com

42. What's the inspiration for the idea?

I see some elderly people. Those of great knowledge and experience. Some wallow in poverty. Some have little income. Some are victims of lack of planning. Some are victims of corruption. Some beg directly or indirectly. Some just watch the days rolling by.

But they probably seat on gold, without them knowing.

They have a wealth of experience which could be turned to cash. Some have marital experiences. Some have work experiences some have parental experiences. Some survived against the odds. Some have spiritual experiences. Some have culinary experiences of very traditional meals which may otherwise go extinct. The list is endless.

Couldn't these experiences be curated by them, or via collaborators? Could they be stand-alone content or content merged with others? Could they be on different platforms and in different languages? Isn't this the marriage of content creation, life experience, technology and entrepreneurism?

Is this a good inspiration?

Or will it cause depression?

What are your thoughts?

jacksempowerment.com. jacklookman.co.uk. jaaloo.com

43. What are the threats to this idea?

Possible threats are:

- Conflict between stakeholders
- Intellectual theft
- Not carrying out due diligence
- Inadequate funding
- Lack of interest in the content
- Status-quo fightback
- Inadequate marketing
- Etc

44. Here is a suggested value chain:

- The story originator (or narrator)
- The Content Creator
- The entrepreneur
- The publisher
- The platforms
- The content consumer
- Generations of content consumers
- Educational institutions
- Legal personnel
- Parents
- Children
- Youths
- Adults
- Etc

jacksempowerment.com. jacklookman.co.uk. jaaloo.com

45. What's the value proposition?

The value on offer is the sharing of life experiences; the good, bad and ugly; for people to benefit.

- To mould opinions.

- To enrich society.
- To avoid unnecessary pitfalls.
- To create income streams
- And to make the world a better place.

46. What does life experience entail?

It entails any activity or observation by humans.

For the purpose of this content, such experience shall be beneficial and add value to generations.

If value is given, entrepreneurial rewards shall follow.

jacksempowerment.com. jacklookman.co.uk. jaaloo.com

47. Who benefits from this venture?

- The story originator (narrator)
- The content creator
- The entrepreneur
- Children
- Youths
- Adults
- Society
- Generations

48. Volume and quality of content

Content shall be:

- Entertaining
- Concise
- Educational
- Of great value
- Qualitative

jacksempowerment.com. jacklookman.co.uk. jaaloo.com

49. Dispensation of financial proceeds

Please consider the undermentioned:

- Stakeholders
- Charity
- Recycling into the business
- Agreement
- Timely dispensation
- Contract
- Effective administration

- Accountability
- Transparency

50. Solo stories or compilations?

When curating content, should it be for one or multiple niches? Should the target demographic be singular or multiple?

It could be either or both. That shall be a judgement call for stakeholders. Think about:

- Economics
- Impact
- Logistics
- Individual stories
- Compilation of short stories
- Or both.

It's a judgement call

jacksempowerment.com. jacklookman.co.uk. jaaloo.com

51. Could I do this business as a side or full hustle?

Again, it's a judgement call. You need to evaluate the time and resources spent, as well as the financial returns. If it's financially viable to sustain your needs and those of dependents, you may consider it as a full hustle.

Otherwise, you may consider doing it as a side hustle.

If there is however little or no return you may reconsider your steps, and either terminate the venture or change your approach and strategy.

jacksempowerment.com.   jacklookman.co.uk.   jaaloo.com

52. Some Budgetary considerations:

- Costing

- Expenses

- Profit

- Loss

- Cash flow

- Planning

- Logistics

- Return on investment

- Pricing

- Funding

- Staffing

- Etc

53. If you make profit, should you Re-invest?

The simple answer is yes. You may however need to decide on the percentage once you get the success formula.

You may invest more resources and improve on your doing. That way, you could multiply your profit and grow the business faster, as well as become more impactful.

jacksempowerment.com. jacklookman.co.uk. jaaloo.com

54. Some costing and pricing thoughts

Think about:

- Time
- Resources
- Money
- Return on investment
- Office
- Logistics
- Human resources
- Equipment
- Costs
- Profit

- Break even period
- Affordability
- Competition
- Value
- Reasonability
- Etc

55. Exit Strategy

Consideration shall be given to an exit strategy. What happens with collaborators in the case of:

• death

• sickness

• conflict

• resignation

• sale of business

• etc

jacksempowerment.com. jacklookman.co.uk. jaaloo.com

56. Conclusion

The whole purpose of this academic exercise is to:

- Optimize life experience
- Add value to society
- Empower willing participants
- Create income streams
- Explore the entrepreneurial opportunity
- Create wealth
- Create jobs
- Minimize direct or indirect begging
- Reduce financial burdens on children
- Create financial independence
- Restore dignity of the participants
- Encourage thinking outside the box
- Stimulate thought processes
- Improve self esteem
- Etc

jacksempowerment.com. jacklookman.co.uk. jaaloo.com

57. About Jack Lookman

- He qualified as an Engineer.
- He has varied work experience in paid and unpaid roles and in different sectors.

- He's currently a Content Creator, Mentor, Affiliate Marketer, multiple Author, Entrepreneur, Collaborator and Volunteer.
- He has experienced life's ups and downs
- He's blessed with children.

58. Books by Jack Lookman

- amazon.co.uk search for Jack Lookman
- https://selar.co/m/jacklookman
- Internet search? Jack Lookman

jacksempowerment.com. jacklookman.co.uk. jaaloo.com

59. Some resources by Jack Lookman

- jacksempowerment.com
- jacklookman.co.uk
- jaaloo.com
- Youtube channel: Jack Lookman
- https://youtube.com/@jacklookman
- Youtube channel: Business Ideas etc
- https://youtube.com/@businessideasetc5620
- Facebook: Jack Lookman
- https://www.facebook.com/jack.lookman.3

- Facebook group: Business Ideas etc
- https://www.facebook.com/groups/353168765939448/?ref=share_group_link
- Facebook group: Menteero
- https://www.facebook.com/groups/empowermentinspirationandsupport/?ref=share_group_link

60. Did you get value?

Did you learn 1 or 2 things? Did it stimulate your thoughts? Could it benefit family or friends?

If yes, please consider liking, sharing, subscribing and reposting content on our Social media platforms.

Also consider purchasing our products and services.

jacksempowerment.com. jacklookman.co.uk. jaaloo.com

61. Transcript

The transcript of the video is at: jacksempowerment.com

Search for:

Jack's Curated Business Idea

And, 'Monetising Life Experience'.

62. Will you like to collaborate?

Does the Jack Lookman brand resonate with you? Will you like to collaborate? If yes, please send an email to: jacklookman@yahoo.co.uk

Use an appropriate subject heading and narrative.

jacksempowerment.com. jacklookman.co.uk. jaaloo.com

63. Will you like to be mentored by Jack Lookman?

If yes, please send an email to: jacklookman@yahoo.co.uk

Use an appropriate subject heading and narrative.

Thank you very much for your time.

This is Olayinka Carew aka Jack Lookman signing off.

Ire o (I wish you blessings)

Ire kabiti (I wish you loads of blessings)

You could also check our websites:

- jacksempowerment.com
- jacklookman.co.uk
- jaaloo.com
- Jack's Mentoring 101: https://www.jacksempowerment.com/products/courses/view/1152633
- Or visit jacksempowerment.com - Jack's Mentoring 101

Some of our Social media platforms are:

Jack Lookman - Facebook profile - https:// www.facebook.com/jack.lookman.3

Facebook group: Business Ideas etc: https:// www.facebook.com/groups/353168765939448/? ref=share_group_link

Youtube channel: Business Ideas etc: https://youtube.com/ @businessideasetc5620

Youtube channel: Jack Lookman: https://youtube.com/ @jacklookman

Our books could be found at:

Amazon: https://www.amazon.co.uk/s?
k=jack+lookman&crid=JF245K3USSKQ&sprefix=,aps,44&ref=n
b_sb_ss_recent_1_0_recent

Or - amazon.co.uk - search for Jack Lookman

Selar: https://selar.co/m/jacklookman

Some collaborations:

Selar: https://selar.co/p/63i7?affiliate=m7u3

Selar: https://selar.co/m/gabrieladeola?affiliate=in78

Bluehost: https://bluehost.sjv.io/eK4Qb1

Fiverr Learn: Fiverr Learn: https://go.fiverr.com/visit/?bta=343856&nci=10353

Get Response: https://www.getresponse.com?a=Eq3vWgPgkw&c=jaaloo

Selar - ebook: https://selar.co/m/PastorVictorDavid?affiliate=qudo

Selar - ebook: https://selar.co/p/wuvj?affiliate=vqc6

18. OTHER PUBLICATIONS BY JACK LOOKMAN LIMITED

1. Despair, Submission, Faith and Hope – Volume 1

2. Despair, Submission, Faith and Hope – Volume 2

3. Monetising Digital Book Reviews

4. E-Commerce For Traditional African Attires

5. Basic Management And Fundraising Tip For Community Groups

6. Monetising A Digital Library

7. Ajo, The App And Opportunities

8. Empowering Orphans, Widows and Widowers

9. Submission, Gratitude, Faith and Hope

10. Oro Ishiti- Indelible Yoruba Words

11. Eid Monetisation by Leveraging Technology

12. What are your thoughts? What is your mindset? - Volume 1

13. What are your thoughts? What is your mindset? - Volume 2

14. Twenty Curated Business Ideas - Volume 1

15. Jaaloo Puzzles - Volume 1

16. Jaaloo Puzzles - Volume 2

17. Beauty Of The Storm

18. Digital Career Guidance App

19. Bath Sponge Project

20. Community Group Monetisation

21. Profit Sharing Formula App

19. About Jack Lookman

Olayinka Carew, aka Jack Lookman is the 1st of 5 Children.
He has 3 children, and an elderly mum. He is resident in the United Kingdom and is of Nigerian origin.

He studied at King's College, Lagos and University of Lagos.
He has varied life and work experiences.
He has been involved in voluntary and paid jobs.
He is dedicating the rest of his life to empowering and inspiring generations.
This is one of his legacy projects.
Though he has health challenges, he does not let that impede his mission and vision.
Even though he studied Engineering in University; his calling is so many miles away from that. He is currently an Entrepreneur, Content Creator, Affiliate Marketer, Volunteer, Collaborator and Mentor.

He is the Director and Owner of Jack Lookman Limited, a registered business in the United Kingdom; and their aim is to empower and inspire generations by leveraging the internet.

This is Olayinka Carew aka Jack Lookman signing off.

Ire o (I wish you blessings)

Ire kabiti (I wish you loads of blessings)

www.ingramcontent.com/pod-product-compliance
Lightning Source LLC
Chambersburg PA
CBHW060007300526
45794CB00003B/1121